# My Amazing Body
# GROWING

**Angela Royston**

Raintree

**www.raintreepublishers.co.uk**
Visit our website to find out more information about **Raintree** books.

To order:
☎ Phone 44 (0) 1865 888112
▤ Send a fax to 44 (0) 1865 314091
▯ Visit the Raintree bookshop at **www.raintreepublishers.co.uk** to browse our catalogue and order online.

First published in Great Britain by Raintree,
Halley Court, Jordan Hill, Oxford OX2 8EJ,
part of Harcourt Education.
Raintree is a registered trademark of Harcourt Education Ltd.

Editorial: Nick Hunter and Catherine Clarke
Design: Kim Saar and Roslyn Broder
Illustrations: Will Hobbs
Picture Research: Maria Joannou and Pete Morris
Production: Jonathan Smith

Originated by Dot Gradations Ltd
Printed and bound in China by South China Printing Company

ISBN 1 844 43385 4 (hardback)
08 07 06 05 04
10 9 8 7 6 5 4 3 2 1

ISBN 1 844 43392 7 (paperback)
09 08 07 06 05
10 9 8 7 6 5 4 3 2 1

**British Library Cataloguing in Publication Data**
Royston, Angela
Growing. - (My Amazing Body)
612.6
A full catalogue record for this book is available from the British Library.

**Acknowledgements**
The publishers would like to thank the following for permission to reproduce photographs:
Alamy Images pp. **18**, **20**, **23**; B. Apicella p. **16**; Bubbles p. **14**; Corbis pp. **6**, **10**, **13** (Michael Prince), **15** (Joe McDonald), **25** (Chuck Savage), **28**; FLPA pp. **11** (Tony Hamblin), **17** (Winfried Wisniewski), **21** (Koos Delport); Pete Morris p. **4**; Science Photo Library pp. **5** (Secchi, Lecaque, Roussel, UCLAF, CNRI), **7** bottom (John Mitchell), **7** top (Gregory Dimijian), **8** (Renee Lynn), **9** (Petit Format/Prof. E. Symonds), **12** (Ian Boddy), **19** (BSIP/VEM), **22** (Jerry Wachter), **24** (BSIP Chassenet), **26** (Biophoto Associates), **27** (BSIP Franken).

Cover photograph of an X-ray of milk and adult teeth, reproduced with permission of Science Photo Library (BSIP/VEM) and of a child smiling reproduced with permission of Alamy Images (Goodshot).

The publishers would like to thank Carol Ballard for her assistance in the preparation of this book.

Every effort has been made to contact copyright holders of any material reproduced in this book. Any omissions will be rectified in subsequent printings if notice is given to the publishers.

The paper used to print this book comes from sustainable resources.

# Contents

Inside and out................................................4

When do I grow? .............................................6

Life before birth .............................................8

How many babies? ........................................10

Walking and talking ......................................12

Growing bigger ............................................14

Brothers and sisters......................................16

A new set of teeth........................................18

Becoming an adult .......................................20

Growing old..................................................22

Healthy growth.............................................24

What can go wrong? ....................................26

The whole body ............................................28

Find out for yourself......................................30

Glossary .......................................................31

Index ...........................................................32

Any words appearing in bold, **like this**, are explained in the Glossary.

# Inside and out

Humans grow from a small baby into a child, and then into an adult. Your body slowly becomes taller, wider and stronger. Your brain **develops** too. You learn to speak, to read and to understand the world around you.

Photos show how you have grown and changed.

## Growing bigger

You can see for yourself how you have grown and changed by looking at photographs of yourself taken a few years ago. Animals grow too. If you have a kitten or a puppy, it will grow into an adult cat or dog.

This is what a cell looks like under a microscope. Cells are normally too small to see. The microscope makes it look thousands of times larger.

## Inside your body

You can see the changes on the outside of your body, but the inside of your body is growing too. Your bones become longer and every bit of the inside of your body becomes bigger. Your body grows by making extra **cells**. Cells are the tiny building blocks that make each part of your body.

# When do I grow?

You grow taller when you are a baby and a child. You stop growing taller when you are about 18 years old. Adults go on changing as they grow older, but they do not grow taller.

This toddler is about half the height of her mother. She still has a lot of growing to do!

## Growing babies

You grew fastest before you were born. Each baby grows from a tiny egg that is about half the size of a grain of salt. When it is born, the baby measures about 50 centimetres. Babies go on growing quickly. By the age of two, a toddler is about half its fully grown height.

## Changing shape

Some animals, such as frogs and some insects, look quite different when they are young from when they are adults. Frogs begin life as tadpoles. A butterfly begins life as a caterpillar.

A butterfly spends much of its life as a caterpillar before it forms a cocoon and changes into an adult butterfly.

## Growth spurts

You do not grow at the same rate all the time. Sometimes you seem to stop growing for several months, and then suddenly you have grown more than a centimetre. Most children have growth spurts, particularly between the ages of ten and sixteen.

Each person and animal begins life as a **fertilized** egg. This egg is a single **cell** that divides over and over again to make millions of new cells. As the cells divide, they form the different parts of the body – the **heart**, **lungs**, brain, bones and **muscles**.

This chick has hatched out of its shell. It pecked a hole from inside the shell and forced it open.

## Birds and reptiles

Birds lay eggs surrounded by shells. Birds sit on their eggs to keep them warm. Inside each egg, the single cell grows into a chick. Most reptiles, such as snakes, lay eggs too.

## Mammals

Cats, dogs, monkeys, whales and people are **mammals**. Mammals do not lay eggs. Instead the egg grows into a baby inside the mother's body. The baby is born when it has developed and grown strong enough to survive.

This X-ray shows a baby growing inside a woman's body.

## World's biggest baby

The blue whale is the largest animal in the world. A newborn baby blue whale weighs about 1800 kilograms. It is nearly as heavy and as long as two cars end to end.

9

# How many babies?

Many animals give birth to several babies at the same time. With humans, too, a mother sometimes gives birth to more than one baby at the same time. Twins are quite common, but sometimes three, four, five or six babies are born.

## Identical twins

Some twins are identical. They are the same **gender** and they look exactly alike. This is because they grew from one egg that split into two. Other twins form from two different eggs. These twins are called 'non-identical' and might be a boy and a girl.

Twins are two brothers or sisters who are born at the same time. These twins are non-identical.

These kittens were born in the same litter but they all look slightly different.

## Animal families

Sheep and cows usually give birth to twins, but some animals produce several babies at the same time. Several baby animals born together are called a litter. For example, dogs have between four and ten puppies in each litter.

### Frogs' eggs

Frogs lay hundreds of eggs at a time, but most are eaten by fish or other animals. Some eggs survive and hatch into tadpoles, but only one or two survive to become frogs.

# Walking and talking

Newborn human babies are almost helpless. They cannot even hold their heads up. Slowly the **muscles** in their necks and backs become stronger so that by the time they are about 6 months old they can sit up on their own. While their bodies become stronger, their brains **develop** too.

Most babies begin to walk when they are about 1 year old. This baby still needs the support of this trolley.

## Learning to walk and talk

Babies begin to walk by first holding on to something, such as a chair, and pulling themselves upright. With practice, the muscles in their legs and back become stronger and they can take their first steps.

Babies babble as they listen to, and try out, different sounds. Around the age of 1 year, toddlers begin to say single words. By the time they are between 3 and 4 years old, most toddlers can talk very well.

Toddlers can understand some words before they are able to speak. They often point to things they want.

## Born to walk

Many animals, including cows, goats and sheep, can walk from the day they are born. They have to be able to move to keep out of danger.

# Growing bigger

As you grow, you get taller and your body changes shape. The shape of your body changes because some bones grow faster than others. As your bones grow, your skin, **muscles** and the **organs** inside your body grow too.

Some parts of the body grow more than others. The boys' heads are not much bigger than the baby's, but their arms are much longer than the baby's arms.

14

## Changing shape

Babies have a large head compared to the rest of their body. As babies and toddlers grow, their arms and legs grow faster than the rest of their body, while their head grows much more slowly.

## How bones grow

Bones form from a rubbery substance called cartilage. The cartilage in bones slowly hardens to form new bone. Even when you are an adult, your bones go on making cartilage at the ends of some of your bones to stop them grinding against each other.

## Snake skin

A snake's thick, scaly skin does not grow as the snake grows. Instead the snake sheds its skin from time to time as it grows, revealing a brand new skin that has grown underneath.

# Brothers and sisters

Children in the same family often look similar. They may have the same shape face or the same hair colour. If you have brothers and sisters, you probably look similar, because some of your features are **inherited** from your parents.

One of these girls has inherited red hair from her mother.

## Colour of eyes

If both of your parents have brown eyes you will probably have brown eyes too. If your parents both have blue eyes, your eyes will probably be blue. The colour of your eyes may be different from your parents' eyes, but your colour will have been passed down from one of your grandparents.

## Height

Height is partly inherited and partly due to the food you usually eat. You need to eat food such as cheese, beans, meat or fish, which have plenty of protein, to grow to your full height.

## You are unique!

Every human and animal is **unique**. Even identical twins have different fingerprints. Zebras look alike to us, but each zebra's stripes form a unique pattern.

# A new set of teeth

Most human babies are born with no teeth. They feed on milk until they are about 14 weeks old, when they start eating soft food. Inside the **gums** is a set of milk teeth, which begin to come through the gums from about the age of 5 or 6 months. At the same time, **permanent** teeth form in the jawbones.

This boy has a permanent tooth at the front of the top of his mouth. The rest of his teeth are milk teeth.

Front teeth are usually the first milk teeth to come through. The larger, back teeth follow later. Then the baby can chew harder food.

## Permanent teeth

When you are about 6 or 7 years old, your milk teeth become loose and begin to fall out. They are partly pushed out by the permanent teeth growing up through the gums. Look after your permanent teeth – they have to last the rest of your life!

This X-ray shows inside a mouth where a permanent tooth (green) is growing up between the roots of the milk teeth.

## Crocodile teeth

Unlike humans, crocodiles have an endless supply of teeth. As one tooth is worn away and falls out, another tooth grows in its place.

Between the ages of about ten and fourteen a child begins to change into an adult. This is called puberty. Puberty usually begins sooner in girls than in boys. The body changes over several years.

## Changing into a woman

During puberty a girl grows taller and the shape of her body becomes more rounded. Hair grows more thickly under her arms, on her legs and between her legs. **Organs** inside her body change so that one day she may be able to have a baby.

Teenagers start to look after themselves, but usually still live with their parents until they are about 18 years old.

# Animal parents

Birds, rabbits and other small animals leave their parents when they are a few months old. Larger animals stay in their families for longer. Female elephants never leave the herd, but young males are forced to leave when they are about 12 years old.

## Changing into a man

Boys also grow taller during puberty and hair grows on their bodies too. A boy's voice becomes much deeper and, later, he begins to grow a beard. Organs inside his body also change so that one day he may be a father.

# Growing old

People's bodies change as they grow older. Their skin becomes wrinkled and they cannot run as fast as they used to. Their hair may gradually become grey, and their eyesight and hearing may not work so well.

## Eyesight and hearing

Many people start to see less clearly when they are about 40–50 years old. Older people often wear glasses for reading and writing. Most elderly people do not hear as well as when they were younger.

People may slow down as they grow older but they can still be fit and active. This couple are jogging through the park.

## Harder to bend and stretch

As people become older, their **joints** become stiffer. This means that they cannot bend their knees and backs so easily. Sometimes their fingers and shoulders become stiffer too.

This dog is clearly quite old. You can see how the hair around its mouth and eyes has gone grey.

## Lifespans of some animals

| Mouse | 2–3 years |
|---|---|
| Rabbit | 12 years |
| Cat | 14 years |
| Horse | 25 years |
| Elephant | 60 years |
| Tortoise | 100 years |

# Healthy growth

The foods you eat may affect how tall you grow and how strong your bones and teeth are. If you eat a wide range of different foods, you should get all the **nutrients** your body needs to grow and stay healthy.

## Healthy food

Your body needs **protein** to make new **cells**. Meat, cheese, fish and beans all contain lots of protein. Cheese, milk and some vegetables contain **calcium**. Calcium makes your bones and teeth strong.

These foods all contain protein and calcium, which help you to grow well. You should eat at least two portions of these foods every day.

24

## Sleep and exercise

Good sleep and plenty of exercise also help you to grow well. You grow fastest when you are asleep! Exercise makes your **muscles** and bones stronger and your **heart** and **lungs** work better.

## Checking growth

Most young children have a regular medical check, when a doctor checks that they are growing well. The doctor measures their height and weight.

The doctor is measuring this boy's height to see how much he has grown since his last medical check.

# What can go wrong?

As long as you eat healthy food you should grow to your full height. If your diet lacks some important foods though, you may suffer from illnesses that affect your growth.

## Lack of protein

If you do not eat food that contains enough **protein** your body will not be able to make as many new **cells** as you need to grow.

This woman's bones are shaped this way because she has rickets.

## Rickets

Milk, cheese, eggs and oily fish contain lots of calcium and vitamin D, which your body needs to form strong bones. Children who do not have enough of these **nutrients** may get a **disease** called rickets. Their bones are soft and their legs may become bent and bandy.

A pregnant woman's health affects the health of her unborn child. Mothers who smoke tobacco can damage the health of their babies.

## Smoking

Mothers who smoke while they are pregnant are more likely than non-smokers to have babies that have not grown enough before they were born. If the mother goes on smoking after the baby is born, the baby is more likely to suffer from chest **infections**.

# The whole body

Different parts of your body work better when you are fit and healthy. If one part of your body is not working well, it causes problems for the rest of your body. For example, to grow tall, your stomach and **intestines** need to work properly, so that **nutrients** from the food you eat can reach the rest of your body.

Exercise is good for your muscles and bones. Taking your weight on your arms helps your arm bones to grow stronger.

## Controlling growth

The part of the body that controls how well you grow is deep in your brain, but each part of your body grows so slowly that you don't notice it.

## Looking good

Every person looks a bit different from everyone else. You look at your best when you are fit, healthy and happy. Your body is very special – think of all the amazing things it can do!

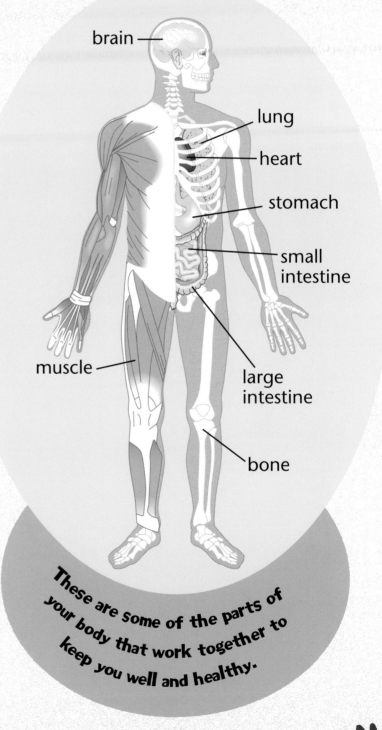

brain

lung

heart

stomach

small intestine

muscle

large intestine

bone

These are some of the parts of your body that work together to keep you well and healthy.

# Find out for yourself

Everybody's body is slightly different but they all work in the same way. Find out more about how your own amazing body works by noticing what happens to it. How many milk teeth have you lost? How much have you grown in the last year? Do you have any brothers or sisters who look like you? You will find the answers to many of your questions in this book, but you can also use other books and the Internet.

## Books to read

*Everyday Science: About Your Body,* Barbara Taylor (Hodder Wayland, 2001)

*My World of Science: Human Growth,* Angela Royston (Heinemann Library, 2003)

## Using the Internet

Explore the Internet to find out more about growing. Websites can change, but if one of the links below no longer works, don't worry. Use a search engine, such as www.yahooligans.com or www.internet4kids.com, and type in keywords such as 'growing up' or 'milk teeth'.

## Websites:

www.kidshealth.org contains lots of information about how your body works and how to stay healthy

www.bbc.co.uk/science/humanbody/body contains an interactive body and lots of information. Click on 'bone growth' and 'growth spurt' to find out more about growing.

## Disclaimer

All the Internet addresses (URLs) given in this book were valid at the time of going to press. However, due to the dynamic nature of the Internet, some addresses may have changed, or sites may have ceased to exist since publication. While the author and publishers regret any inconvenience this may cause readers, no responsibility for any such changes can be accepted by either the author or the publishers.

**calcium** chemical that your body uses to grow strong bones and teeth

**cell** smallest building block of living things

**develop** grow and change

**disease** illness

**fertilized** able to grow into a new person or animal. A female egg is fertilized when it is joined by a male cell.

**fingerprint** pattern made by the skin on the tip of the thumb or fingers

**gender** male or female (boy or girl)

**gum** flesh that covers the jawbones inside your mouth

**heart** special muscle in your chest that pumps blood around your body

**hip** joint where the top of the thigh bone meets the rest of the body

**infection** illness caused by germs

**inherit** get from your parents or grandparents

**intestine** long tube that carries waste from your stomach to the outside of your body

**joint** place where two bones meet

**lungs** parts of the body that take in oxygen when you breathe in and get rid of waste carbon dioxide when you breathe out

**mammal** group of animals that feed their babies on mother's milk

**microscope** instrument that makes very tiny things look large enough to see

**muscles** parts of the body that you use to move

**nutrients** parts of food that your body needs to stay healthy

**organ** part of the body, such as the heart, brain and stomach, that has a particular job to do

**permanent** lasting

**protein** nutrients that your body needs to grow new cells and repair damaged cells

**unique** only one

**vitamin** chemicals found in some foods that your body needs to stay healthy

**X-ray** kind of photograph that shows parts of the inside of your body, such as your bones and the roots of your teeth

# Index

adults 4, 6, 15, 20, 22–23
animals 5, 7, 8, 9, 10, 11, 13, 15, 17, 19, 21, 23

babies and toddlers 6, 7, 9, 10, 12–13, 15, 18, 20, 27
birds 8, 9
blue whale 9
bones 8, 15, 24, 25, 26, 27, 28
brain 4, 8, 12, 29
brothers and sisters 10, 16

calcium 24, 27
cells 5, 8, 24, 26
crocodiles 19

eggs 7, 8, 9, 10, 11
elephants 21, 23
exercise 22, 25, 28
eye colour 17
eyesight 22

food, healthy 17, 24–25, 26, 27

growth spurts 7

hair 16, 20, 21, 22
head 14, 15
hearing 22
heart and lungs 8, 25
height 6, 7, 17, 25

inside your body 5, 29

joints 23

lifespans 23

mammals 9
medical checks 25
muscles 8, 12, 13, 14, 25, 28

nutrients 24, 27, 28

old, growing 22–23

pregnant women 27
problems, health 26–27, 28
protein 17, 24, 26
puberty 20, 21

rickets 26, 27

shape, changing 7, 14–15, 20
smoking 27
snakes 9, 15

teenagers 20
teeth 18–19, 24
twins 10–11, 17

walking and talking 12, 13
whole body 28–29